Design
and
compilations
by
D'Bee

Sources: Bartleby.com, brainyquote.com, famousquotes.com, famousquotesandauthors. com, goodquotes.com, goodreads.com, notable-quotes.com, quotationspage.com, quotationsbook.com, quote-museum.com, quotesdaddy.com, searchquotes.com, thinkexist.com, wikiquote.org, Google Books, Oxford Dictionary of Modern Quotations, The Oxford Dictionary of Quotations, In Praise of the Shadows (1933).

A portion of the proceeds from this book is allocated to charity.

For friends and family

Gravitation is not responsible
for those falling in love.

Albert Einstein

Love is metaphysical gravity.

R. Buckminster Fuller

A kiss is a rosy dot over the 'i' of loving.

Cyrano de Bergerac

Love is composed

of a single soul inhabiting two bodies.

Aristotle

Unity itself

and the idea of Unity

are already two.

Buddha

Love is only a dirty trick
played on us to achieve continuation of the species.

W. Somerset Maugham

Horse sense

is the thing a horse has

which keeps it

from betting on people.

W. C. Fields

A kiss is a lovely trick
designed by nature
to stop speech
when words become
superfluous.

Ingrid Bergman

Love is a game that two can play and both win.

Eva Gabor

With the catching

ends the pleasure of the chase.

Abraham Lincoln

It's good sportsmanship

to not pick up lost golf balls while they are still rolling.

Mark Twain

By practicing

reverence

for life

we become

good,

deep,

and alive.

Albert Schweitzer

Throw

your dreams

into space

like a kite,

and you

do not know

what

it will bring back,

a new life,

a new friend,

a new love,

a new country.

Anais Nin

Come live in my heart,

and pay no rent.

Samuel Lover

At the
touch of love
everyone
becomes a poet.

Plato

A single act of kindness

throws out roots

in all directions,

and the roots spring up

and make new trees.

Amelia Earhart

Find beauty

not only in the thing itself

but in the pattern of the shadows,

the light and dark

which that thing provides.

Junichiro Tanizaki

Love is a canvas
furnished by nature and
embroidered
by imagination.

Voltaire

Friendship is

Love without his wings.

Lord Byron

A friend is one

who has the same enemies

as you have.

Abraham Lincoln

Love is being stupid together.

Paul Valery

If we could be twice young

and twice old,

we could correct all

our mistakes.

Euripides

When you
look into an abyss,
the abyss
also looks into you.

Friedrich Nietzsche

A true friend

never gets in your way

unless you

happen to be going down.

Arnold H. Glasow

A friend is,

as it were,

a second self.

Marcus Tullius Cicero

The lovesick,

the betrayed, and the jealous all smell alike.

Sidonie Gabrielle Colette

It takes
one to forgive,
it takes
two to be reunited.

Lewis B. Smedes

One loyal friend is worth ten thousand relatives.

Euripides

Each friend
represents a world
in us,
a world not born
until they arrive, and
it is only
by this meeting
that a new world
is born.

Anais Nin

If evolution really works,
how come mothers only
have two hands?

Milton Berle

A very small degree of hope

is sufficient to cause the birth of love.

Stendhal

If you treat your wife like a thoroughbred, you'll never end up with a nag.

Zig Ziglar

Each child is

an adventure into a better life

an opportunity to

change the old pattern and

make it new.

Hubert H. Humphrey

A true friend

is someone who thinks that

you are a good egg

even though he knows that

you are slightly cracked.

Bernard Meltzer

"Stay" is a charming word in a friend's vocabulary.

Louisa May Alcott

In every living thing there is
the desire for love.

David Herbert Lawrence

Without deep reflection
one knows from daily life that one exists for others.

Albert Einstein

A loving heart

is the beginning of all knowlege.

Thomas Carlyle

Quotes
for Life®